THE
BATHROOM
GOLF BOOK

by

Harry Patterson

RED-LETTER PRESS, INC.
Saddle River, New Jersey

For information address:

Red-Letter Press, Inc.
P.O. Box 393, Saddle River, NJ 07458
www.Red-LetterPress.com

ACKNOWLEDGMENTS

Project Development Coordinator:
Kobus Reyneke

Cover design and typography:
s.w.artz, inc.

Editorial:
Jack Kreismer

Significant Others:
Jarret Hillman, Kathy Hoyt, Mike Ryan, Remi Walsh

Special Thanks To:
Ian Rodgers, Cousin Chris Patterson, Bob Cascella,
The staff at the Shaler North Hills Library,
The gang at the Shaler Lounge,
and as always, The gang at the River City Inn

INTRODUCTION

For more than twenty years, the original Bathroom Library has entertained people "on the go" everywhere.
With millions of copies out there, it proves that we're not all wet about bathroom reading.

Now, as heir to the throne, we proudly introduce a brand new Bathroom Library. We hope you enjoy this installment of it.

Yours flushingly,

Jack Kreismer
Publisher

FOR AMERICA'S
FAVORITE READING ROOM

THE
BATHROOM
GOLF BOOK

*Quips and Quizzes
for the 19th Hole*

THE BATHROOM LIBRARY

RED-LETTER PRESS, INC.
Saddle River, New Jersey

FIRST OF ALL

1. Who was the first to win all four modern majors?

2. When was the US Open first televised?

3. Who was the first to win four LPGA majors in a career?

4. Who was the first to reach $100,000 career winnings in a single season?

5. What was the first year admission was charged for the US Open—1922, 1932, 1942 or 1952?

6. Who was the first British monarch to attend the British Open? (Hint: It was 1948.)

7. Which major is the first one played in the calendar year?

8. Who was America's first golf pro—that is, he made his living solely by playing golf?

9. Who was the first black player to qualify for the Masters?

10. Who was the first to play four sub-70 rounds at the US Open?

ANSWERS

1. Gene Sarazen

2. 1954

3. Pat Bradley

4. Arnold Palmer (1963)

5. 1922

6. King George V

7. The Masters (April)

8. Walter Hagen

9. Lee Elder (He missed the cut.)

10. Lee Trevino (1968)

CHIP SHOT

The follow-through is that part of the golf swing
that takes place after the ball has been struck but
before the club has been thrown.

-Henry Beard

ARNIE

He is the first of only four players to rate a page of his own.
How much do you know about Arnold Palmer?

1. What was Arnold Palmer's very first pro tournament win?

2. He won the 1960 US Open in Denver with a 65 on the final round. How many strokes behind was he after three rounds?

3. He was named AP Athlete of the Decade and *Sports Illustrated* Sportsman of the Year. Do you know which decade and year?

4. What up-and-comer beat Arnie in an 18 hole playoff to win the 1962 US Open?

5. Arnie won all the majors except the PGA. Was he ever a runner-up in that tournament?

6. During which year did he become the very first golfer to reach one million dollars in career winnings? Was it 1964, 1966, 1968 or 1972?

7. Long after winning his last major he continued to rank high on the list of highest paid athletes when what variable is factored in?

8. How many US Senior Opens did he play in before winning?

9. What is his home course?

10. Did his wife ever appear on *The Tonight Show*?

ANSWERS

1. The 1955 Canadian Open—He won $2000.

2. Seven

3. AP—1960-69; SI—1960

4. Nicklaus

5. Yes—in 1964, 1968 and 1970 (tied for second in all three)

6. 1968

7. Outside the ropes income such as endorsements, appearance fees and business interests

8. He won in his very first try.

9. Latrobe Country Club

10. NO! Shame on you if you ever fell for that one.

CHIP SHOT

In golf, when we hit a foul ball,
we've got to go out there and play it.

-Sam Snead, comparing golf to baseball

MELTING POT

Match the golfer with the country he or she is from.

1. Gary Player	A. USA
2. Vijay Singh	B. Scotland
3. Greg Norman	C. Spain
4. Seve Ballesteros	D. South Africa
5. Nick Faldo	E. Argentina
6. Bob Charles	F. Puerto Rico
7. Chi Chi Rodriguez	G. New Zealand
8. Tommy Armour	H. Fiji
9. Roberto Di Vicenzo	I. Australia
10. Michelle Wie	J. England

ANSWERS

1. D (Player-South Africa)

2. H (Singh-Fiji)

3. I (Norman-Australia)

4. C (Ballesteros-Spain)

5. J (Faldo-England)

6. G (Charles-New Zealand)

7. F (Rodriguez-Puerto Rico—OK not really a country)

8. B (Armour-Scotland)

9. E (Di Vicenzo-Argentina

10. A (Wie-USA)

CHIP SHOT

I'm one under. One under a tree, one under a rock,
one under a bush...

-Pro hockey goalie *Gary Cheevers*

BY ANY OTHER NAME

The answers to the following are not generally known by their given first names, which are provided in the clues.

1. Mary Katherine had the lowest scoring average in the LPGA in each season from 1960-64.

2. Eternal amateur Charles' greatest legacy is the Evans Scholarship for caddies, established in 1930 and accounting for more than 5000 college graduates.

3. In 1979 Severino, 22, became the youngest winner of the British Open since 1893.

4. In 1994 Frank set a record by winning more money without winning a tournament than any other player at that time.

5. William set a record when he logged a 30 on the back nine during the 1967 Masters.

6. In 1945 John won 11 PGA Tour events in a row.

7. Juan had eight PGA Tour victories, but his game (and his popularity) exploded on the Senior Tour which he became eligible for in 1985.

8. Eldrick won three US Amateurs and an NCAA Championship.

9. Alexander was the first British player to win the Masters.

10. Mildred was an all-around athlete who excelled not only at golf but also swimming, basketball, bowling, track and tennis among others.

ANSWERS

1. Mickey Wright

2. Chick Evans

3. Seve Ballesteros

4. Fuzzy Zoeller

5. Ben Hogan (Benjamin is his middle name.)

6. Byron Nelson (Byron is his middle name.)

7. Chi Chi Rodriguez

8. Tiger Woods

9. Sandy Lyle

10. Babe Didrikson Zaharias

CHIP SHOT

Jimmy Demaret and I had the best sports psychologist
in the world. His name was Jack Daniels and
he was waiting for us after every round.

-Jackie Burke

OF COURSES

Each of the following refers to a well known golf course.

1. Golf has been played at these Scottish links for over 400 years, including more than two dozen British Opens.

2. Robert Trent Jones was called upon to make alterations to this course near Detroit for the 1951 US Open.

3. One of several "Royal" clubs to host the British Open, this one was awarded its royal charter in 1978, its centenary year.

4. This relatively new Ontario course opened for play in 1975 and is regularly rated the best in Canada.

5. This Jack Nicklaus-designed course in Ohio was named for the Scottish links where he won his first British Open.

6. There are five public courses located in this New York State Park, known as the Blue, Yellow, Red, Green and, yes, Black.

7. It is the only public course to host multiple US Opens.

8. In 1987 it became the only golf course to be designated a National Historic Landmark.

9. Wicker baskets are used atop the pins at this course near Philadelphia.

10. Each hole is named after one of the many shrubs, trees or flowers on the course (Redbud, Holly, Magnolia, etc.)

ANSWERS

1. St. Andrews
2. Oakland Hills
3. Royal Troon
4. The National
5. Muirfield Village
6. Bethpage
7. Pebble Beach
8. Oakmont
9. Merion
10. Augusta National

CHIP SHOT

Golf is a game in which one endeavors to control a ball with implements ill-adapted for the purposes.

-Woodrow Wilson

LINKS LINGO

Can you come up with the golf terms from these definitions?

1. The number of strokes a player receives to adjust his scoring level to a common level of even par

2. Competition decided by the winner of the hole, regardless of the number of strokes

3. A more formal name for stroke play, where the outcome is decided by the total number of strokes

4. Three over par on a single hole

5. To hit a ball to the right of the intended target area

6. To hit a ball to the left of the intended target area

7. The position that a player takes while preparing to start a stroke

8. The player (or the ball) farthest from the hole, who plays next

9. The British term for a double eagle

10. A person, usually a volunteer, appointed by the tournament committee to help keep order and facilitate crowd control

ANSWERS

1. Handicap
2. Match play
3. Medal play
4. Triple bogey
5. Slice
6. Hook
7. Address
8. Away
9. Albatross
10. Marshal

CHIP SHOT

Combination rest home and gold mine.

-*Dan Jenkins*, about the Senior Tour

THEY PLAYED TOO

They'll never be up there with Jack, Arnie or Tiger, but each of the following made his mark on (or, in one case, way way off) the golf course in one way or another. Identify the following.

1. I wanna tell you. He was one of the greatest entertainers of the 20th century before his death at 100 in the 21st Century. He was also one of golf's most enthusiastic boosters and once boasted a four handicap. And how 'bout that Desert Classic?

2. He was NFL MVP in 1970 before stopping off at the broadcast booth and moving on to the PGA Senior Tour years after that.

3. He was the world heavyweight champion boxer for 12 years, as well as a pretty decent golfer, despite being forced to play mostly on inferior public courses because of his race.

4. This diminutive goodfella has long been a crowd favorite at celebrity and charity events.

5. This Hockey Hall of Famer's charity tournament near Pittsburgh is rapidly becoming the golf event for athletes from other sports.

6. He is a basketball legend and a baseball washout. Golf just may be his second best sport.

7. In 1971 he left a solid baseball career (A's, Senators, Red Sox, Indians) to try a pro golf career. It didn't happen.

8. This former major league pitcher (Yankees, Pirates) moved on to become the top money winner in celebrity golf.

9. He famously played the groundskeeper in *Caddyshack* and also played in quite a few celebrity and charity events.

10. He was the first American in space and the first to hit a golf ball on the moon.

ANSWERS

1. Bob Hope
2. John Brodie
3. Joe Louis
4. Joe Pesci
5. Mario Lemieux
6. Michael Jordan
7. Ken Harrelson
8. Rick Rhoden
9. Bill Murray
10. Alan Shepard (He used a six iron.)

CHIP SHOT

Golf is like a love affair: if you don't take it seriously,
it's no fun; if you do take it seriously, it breaks your heart.

-Arnold Daly

NO, NOT HIM

Can you identify each of the following golfers,
all of whom appeared on the scene with names that
were already somewhat familiar?

1. Not the director of The *Treasure of Sierra Madre* and
   Chinatown, but the guy with six PGA Tour victories and two
   stints on the Presidents Cup team (1994 and 1998).

2. Not the legendary athlete played by Burt Lancaster in a movie,
   but the 2002 winner of The Tradition.

3. Not the creator of the cartoon *Beany and Cecil*, but the CBS
   golf reporter and former pro.

4. Not Gracie's husband, but the guy who tied for second at the
   1981 US Open behind winner David Graham following a
   three stroke lead after the third round.

5. Not the four-time winner of the Boston Marathon, but the
   other guy who tied for second at the 1981 US Open (see above).

6. Not the father of Greg, Bobby and Peter (or the stepfather of
   Marsha, Jan and Cindy), but the guy who twice lost the
   US Open in playoffs (1911 and 1919) and never won the event.

7. Not the British talk show host who interviewed Nixon, but the
   guy who birdied the final hole to win the 1993 Canadian Open.

8. Not the host of *What's My Line?*, but the winner of the 1995
   British Open.

9. Not the guitarist for the Sex Pistols, but the winner of the
   1996 US Open.

10. Not the former Cincinnati Bengals All-Pro defensive lineman,
    but the guy who lost the 1989 PGA to Payne Stewart after
    leading by two strokes with three holes left to play.

ANSWERS

1. John Huston
2. Jim Thorpe
3. Bobby Clampett
4. George Burns
5. Bill Rogers
6. Mike Brady
7. David Frost
8. John Daly
9. Steve Jones
10. Mike Reid

CHIP SHOT

Most people play like Magellan.
They're all over the world.

-Bob Toski

TIGER

He's one of only four players to rate a page of his own.
How much do you know about Tiger Woods?

1. For what university did he win the NCAA title?

2. In 1997 he became the youngest to win the Masters. Who previously held that distinction?

3. Who is Vuong Dang Phong?

4. When he won the Masters was it on his first, second or third attempt?

5. What was his very first pro win?

6. At what age did he first become a scratch golfer? Was it 10, 13, 15 or 16?

7. He was *Sports Illustrated* Sportsman of the Year for 1996 and 2000. Did anyone else ever make it twice?

8. Against whom was he paired for the "Showdown at Sherwood," the very first live network prime time golf telecast?

9. His 19-under 269 at the 2000 British Open set a tournament course record at which venerable venue?

10. Arnold Palmer was the first golfer to reach one million dollars in career earnings. It took him about 14 years. What round number career earnings milestone did Tiger reach in early 1994, after a little less than ten years?

ANSWERS

1. Stanford

2. Seve Ballesteros

3. A Vietnamese soldier, nicknamed "Tiger," after whom Earl Woods nicknamed his son

4. Third

5. The 1996 Greater Milwaukee Open (He won $2,544.)

6. 13

7. No

8. David Duval

9. St. Andrews

10. 40 million

CHIP SHOT

I never exaggerate. I just remember big.

-Chi Chi Rodriguez

"THE" NICKNAMES

Can you identify the players known by "the" following nicknames?

1. The Shark

2. The Walrus

3. The Golden Bear

4. The Squire

5. Gene The Machine

6. The Silver Scott

7. The Hawk

8. The Desert Fox

9. The Lion

10. The King

ANSWERS

1. Greg Norman
2. Craig Stadler
3. Jack Nicklaus
4. Gene Sarazen
5. Gene Littler
6. Tommy Armour
7. Ben Hogan
8. Johnny Miller
9. John Daly
10. Arnold Palmer

CHIP SHOT

I would like to think of myself as an athlete first,
but I don't want to do a disservice to the real ones.

-David Duval

GREENS TO SCREENS

These all deal with golf in the movies.

1. Actor Jim Caviezel played Bobby Jones in a 2004 biopic. Earlier that year he played what other role that garnered him considerably more attention?

2. Name the 1996 comedy that saw the title character get into a golf course fist fight with game show host Bob Barker (as himself).

3. Name the 1953 Martin and Lewis movie which featured Jerry in the title role and Dean singing his hit *That's Amore*.

4. Name the golf legend played by Glenn Ford in 1951's *Follow the Sun*.

5. Which 2000 film (directed by Robert Redford) featured an unbilled cameo by Jack Lemmon that turned out to be his final screen appearance?

6. Which James Bond movie featured a golf match between 007 and the titular villain?

7. Who played Roy "Tin Cup" McAvoy's (Kevin Costner) caddy in *Tin Cup*? Was it Cheech or Chong?

8. Robert Wagner played the title role in which 1967 movie about a golf hustler/ladies man that also featured a fresh-from-Bonnie-and-Clyde Gene Hackman?

9. Name the real life husband and wife who played George Zaharias and Babe Didrikson Zaharias in the 1975 TV movie *Babe*.

10. Name the 1952 Spencer Tracy/Katherine Hepburn vehicle in which Kate plays an all around athlete who golfs against Babe Didrikson Zaharias (in a cameo).

ANSWERS

1. Jesus in *The Passion of the Christ*
2. *Happy Gilmore*
3. *The Caddy*
4. Ben Hogan
5. *The Legend of Bagger Vance*
6. *Goldfinger*
7. Cheech Marin
8. *Banning*
9. Alex Karras and Susan Clark
10. *Pat and Mike*

CHIP SHOT

By the time a man can afford to lose a golf ball,
he can't hit that far.

-Jacob Braude

WHAT'S YOUR MAJOR?

How much do you know about golf's majors?

1. Put the four majors in the order founded, beginning with the oldest.

2. What is the governing body of the British Open?

3. ...the US Open?

4. ...the PGA Championship?

5. ...the Masters?

6. Which of the majors is played on the same course every year?

7. Name the made-for-TV event first played in 1962 that brought together the winners of the four majors.

8. At what course was that event held?

9. In 2000, the Women's British Open was designated as one of the four women's majors. Which tournament did it displace?

10. Name the three other women's majors.

ANSWERS

1. British Open (1860), US Open (1895), PGA (1916), Masters (1934)

2. The Royal and Ancient Golf Club

3. The United States Golf Association

4. The Professional Golfers' Association

5. Augusta National Golf Club

6. The Masters

7. *The World Series of Golf*

8. Firestone Country Club in Akron, Ohio

9. The du Maurier Classic

10. The LPGA, the US Women's Open and the Nabisco Championship

---

CHIP SHOT

I used to shoot my age. Now I would just like to shoot my temperature.

-Jerry Feliciotto

JACK

How much do you know about Jack Nicklaus?

1. How old was Jack when he qualified for his first US Open?

2. He won an unprecedented and unsurpassed 18 major tournaments. Can you break that down into the number of victories in each? (Hint: The numbers are 3, 4, 5 and 6.)

3. How many times was he runner-up in a major?

4. Jack is founder and host of the PGA Tour event The Memorial, which began in 1976. How many times did he win it himself?

5. What year was he named *Sports Illustrated* Sportsman of the Year? Was it 1962, 1966, 1978 or 1986?

6. He won his very first Senior Tour event (The Tradition) in 1990 then headed off to the Masters the following week. Where did he finish?

7. He was the highest ranked golfer on ESPN's 100 Greatest Athletes of the Century. Where did he place? Was it 9th, 15th, 19th or 22nd?

8. On which university campus can the Jack Nicklaus Museum be found?

9. Only one player has recorded more PGA Tour career wins than Nicklaus' 73. Who was it?

10. Who was his caddy when he won the 1986 Masters?

ANSWERS

1. 17 (He missed the cut.)

2. Three British Opens, four US Opens, five PGAs and six Masters

3. 19

4. Twice, in 1977 and 1984

5. 1978

6. Sixth

7. 9th, with only Michael Jordan, Babe Ruth, Muhammad Ali, Jim Brown, Wayne Gretzky, Jesse Owens, Jim Thorpe and Willie Mays (1-8) ahead of him

8. Ohio State

9. Sam Snead with 81

10. His son, Jack

CHIP SHOT

I'm glad we don't have to play in the shade.

-Bobby Jones, when told it was 105 degrees in the shade

FORE TO THE CHIEF

See what you know about The Leader of the Free World hitting a few.

1. Who was the first sitting president to play golf while in office?

2. Which president was a personal friend of Bobby Jones and a dues paying member at Augusta National?

3. Name the successful presidential candidate who resigned under pressure from Baltustrol Golf Club before the election because of the club's exclusion of blacks and females.

4. In 1993 President Clinton and former Presidents Ford and Bush became the first three presidents to play a round of golf together. Who completed the foursome? (Hint: He was neither a politician nor a pro.)

5. Who was the future politician (and Kennedy in-law) who bought President Kennedy's MacGregor Woods golf clubs for $772,500 at the celebrated 1996 auction?

6. Which president underwent emergency surgery following a late night fall at the Florida estate of Greg Norman?

7. There were only three presidents in the 20th century who never picked up a golf club. Hoover and Truman were two. Who was the most recent? (Hint: He preferred softball.)

8. He was the best of the golfer presidents but ironically did not want his game publicized to avoid comparisons to his predecessor who played over a hundred rounds a year during his time in office. Who are we talking about?

9. Who was the first sitting president to play in a Pro-Am event?

10. Which president's administration oversaw a public works program that built over 250 federally funded municipal golf courses, making the sport accessible to hundreds of thousands of new players?

ANSWERS

1. William Howard Taft

2. Dwight Eisenhower

3. Richard Nixon (1968)

4. Bob Hope (at the Bob Hope Chrysler Classic)

5. Arnold Schwarzenegger

6. Bill Clinton

7. Jimmy Carter

8. John F. Kennedy

9. Gerald Ford (Jackie Gleason Inverrary Classic, February 1975)

10. Franklin D. Roosevelt

CHIP SHOT

I played so bad, I got a get-well card from the IRS.

-Johnny Miller, on his disastrous 1977 season

CADDYSHACK

If you're a fan of *Caddyshack*, one of the funniest movies
ever made (that just happens to involve golf), proceed.
If not, go rent the movie and come back.

1. What is the name of the country club?

2. What kind of candy bar was in the pool?

3. What did the Dalai Lama promise Carl Spackler in lieu of a tip?

4. Name the pro golfer who spoofed *Caddyshack* in a 2004
   American Express TV ad.

5. Ty Webb is the only character in both *Caddyshack* and the
   regrettable *Caddyshack II*. Name the actor who played him
   in both.

6. Which two cast members are brothers?

7. What is Judge Smails' first name?

8. Who was the director of *Caddyshack*? (Hint: He also helmed
   Groundhog Day and *Analyze This* and acted in *Stripes* and
   Ghostbusters.)

9. Who performs the song *I'm Alright* on the soundtrack?

10. What is Danny Noonan's final putt worth after Al Czervik gets
    Judge Smails to go double or nothing?

ANSWERS

1. Bushwood

2. Baby Ruth

3. "Total consciousness" on his deathbed

4. Tiger Woods

5. Chevy Chase

6. Bill Murray (Carl Spackler) and Brian Doyle-Murray (Lou Loomis)

7. Elihu

8. Harold Ramis

9. Kenny Loggins

10. $80,000

CHIP SHOT

Gimme: An agreement between two losers who can't putt.

-Jim Bishop

WHO'S HE TALKING ABOUT?

Here are ten quotes and the person quoted. Can you figure out whom each was talking about? Some names may appear more than once.
Hint: One name appears three times.

1. "Now that the big guy's out of the cage, everybody better run for cover."—Arnold Palmer

2. "[He] is the greatest golfer who ever lived and probably ever will live."—Jack Nicklaus

3. "When [he] went, all the other Americans went too, and the British Open was restored to its former majesty."—USGA Executive Director Frank Hannigan

4. "Watching him practice hitting golf balls is like watching fish practice swimming." —John Schlee

5. "He may not be the greatest competitive golfer of all time (though he did win eight major championships), but he is certainly the most popular and beloved of all time."
—golf writer Michael Corcoran

6. "He's a pretty good golfer and he could be much better if he could find more time to play. But I hope he doesn't. I'd rather he be a good president than a good golfer."—Dave Stockton

7. "You look at Bobby Jones and what he did was amazing. Then you look at Jack Nicklaus, and that was amazing too. But when you look at [him], there's been nothing like it in history." —Johnny Miller

8. "In my view, she is the best golfer, male or female, there is. She has a better swing than Tiger Woods."—Peter Thomson

9. "He would do 50 one-armed pushups with me on his back."
—a son on his legendary father's fitness regimen

10. "He knows how to deal with people. He's probably the greatest people person in the history of golf."—Mark O'Meara

ANSWERS

1. Jack Nicklaus

2. Bobby Jones

3. Arnold Palmer

4. Sam Snead

5. Arnold Palmer

6. Gerald Ford

7. Tiger Woods

8. Karrie Webb

9. Jack Snead on father Sam

10. Arnold Palmer

CHIP SHOT

If you can smile when all around you have lost their heads
- you must be the caddie.

-Mike Ryan

MELTING POT II

Again, match the golfer with the country he or she was born in.
This time, one answer is used twice.

1. Anikka Sorenstam   A. Australia

2. Jesper Parnevik   B. Sweden

3. Paul Azinger   C. New Zealand

4. Bob Charles   D. South Africa

5. Laura Davies   E. Spain

6. Ernie Els   F. Scotland

7. Sergio Garcia   G. Germany

8. David Graham   H. England

9. Bernhard Langer   I. USA

10. Colin Montgomerie

ANSWERS

1. B (Sorenstam-Sweden)

2. B (Parnevik-Sweden)

3. I (Azinger-USA)

4. C (Charles-New Zealand)

5. H (Davies-England)

6. D (Els-South Africa)

7. E (Garcia-Spain)

8. A (Graham-Australia)

9. G (Langer-Germany)

10. F (Montgomerie-Scotland)

CHIP SHOT

The safest place would be in the fairway.

-Joe Garagiola, describing the best place for spectators to stand during celebrity golf tournaments

QUOTABLES

Name the person quoted in each of the following.
One is quoted three times here. He's quoted a lot.

1. "People have always been telling what I can't do. I guess I have wanted to show them."

2. "How could they get a picture of me in New York. I ain't never been there." (after seeing his picture in a New York newspaper)

3. "I love Merion and I don't even know her last name." (after winning the US Open there)

4. "My goal was to be the greatest athlete who ever lived."

5. "During a thunderstorm I pull out my one iron, because even God can't hit a one iron."

6. "It took me 17 years to get 3,000 hits. I did it in one afternoon on the golf course."

7. "You're only here for a short visit. Don't hurry, don't worry and be sure to smell the flowers along the way."

8. "Pressure? Pressure is playing a match for ten bucks when you only have five in your pocket."

9. "Golf is a good walk spoiled."

10. "You've got just one problem. You stand too close to the ball—after you've hit it."

ANSWERS

1. Ben Hogan (after his comeback)

2. Sam Snead

3. Lee Trevino

4. Babe Didrikson Zaharias

5. Lee Trevino

6. Hank Aaron

7. Walter Hagen

8. Lee Trevino

9. Mark Twain

10. Sam Snead

CHIP SHOT

There is no movement in the golf swing so difficult
that it cannot be made even more difficult by
careful study and diligent practice.

-Thomas Mulligan

TEE TOMES

Here are ten golf books and ten authors. Match 'em up.

1. *Getting Up and Down:
   My 60 Years in Golf*

2. *Confessions of a Hooker*

3. *How I Play Golf*

4. *I Call the Shots:
   Straight Talk About the
   Game of Golf Today*

5. *Cinderella Story:
   My Life in Golf*

6. *Bogey Man*

7. *Dead Solid Perfect*

8. *Golf My Way*

9. *Golf for Enlightenment:
   The Seven Lessons
   for the Game of Life*

10. *The Legend of Bagger Vance*

A. Deepak Chopra

B. George Plimpton

C. Bill Murray

D. Ken Venturi

E. Steven Pressfield

F. Jack Nicklaus

G. Dan Jenkins

H. Johnny Miller

I. Tiger Woods

J. Bob Hope

ANSWERS

1. D (Venturi)

2. J (Hope)

3. I (Woods)

4. H (Miller)

5. C (Murray)

6. B (Plimpton)

7. G (Jenkins)

8. F (Nicklaus)

9. A (Chopra)

10. E (Pressfield)

CHIP SHOT

I played as much golf as I could in North Dakota,
but summer up there is pretty short.
It usually falls on Tuesday.

-Mike Morley

YES, BUT....

The first five won all but one major. The last five, all but two.
Can you name the majors each did not win?

1. Sam Snead

2. Walter Hagen

3. Byron Nelson

4. Lee Trevino

5. Tom Watson

6. Seve Ballesteros

7. Billy Casper

8. Nick Faldo

9. Johnny Miller

10. Nick Price

ANSWERS

1. Snead—US Open

2. Hagen—Masters

3. Nelson—British Open

4. Trevino—Masters

5. Watson—PGA

6. Ballesteros—US Open, PGA

7. Casper—British Open, PGA

8. Faldo—Masters, PGA

9. Miller—Masters, PGA

10. Price—Masters, US Open

CHIP SHOT

Man blames fate for other accidents but feels personally responsible for a hole in one.

-Martha Beckman

THE YEAR WAS….

Give the year for each of the following headlines.

1. TIGER WINS US OPEN BY 15 STROKES

2. BEN HOGAN SERIOUSLY INJURED IN AUTO ACCIDENT

3. NICKLAUS WINS BACK-TO-BACK MASTERS TITLES

4. FINSTERWALD WINS PGA—FIRST UNDER STROKE PLAY

5. GOLF LEGEND BOBBY JONES DEAD AT 69

6. NICKLAUS WINS SECOND US AMATEUR

7. TONY LEMA DIES IN PLANE CRASH

8. NORMAN TAKES BRITISH OPEN—267 LOWEST SCORE IN 122 YEAR HISTORY

9. BYRON NELSON WINS 11TH CONSECUTIVE TOURNAMENT

10. HAGEN WINS FOURTH STRAIGHT PGA

ANSWERS

1. 2000
2. 1949
3. 1966
4. 1958
5. 1971
6. 1961
7. 1966
8. 1993
9. 1945
10. 1927

CHIP SHOT

I must say, my pal Charley (Pride) hit some good
woods… most of them were trees.

-Glen Campbell

AGES FOR THE AGES

Give the age of each of the following at the point indicated within a year—that is, you can be one over or one under and still be considered correct.

1. Tiger Woods when he won the 1997 Masters

2. Jack Nicklaus when he won his sixth and final Masters

3. Gene Sarazen when he died in 1999

4. Tiger when he putted with Bob Hope on *The Mike Douglas Show*

5. John Daly when he won the 1995 British Open

6. Arnold Palmer when Jack Nicklaus beat him in a playoff for the US Open

7. Bobby Jones when he retired from competitive golf

8. Sam Snead when he won his final PGA Tour event (Greater Greensboro Open)

9. Ben Crenshaw when he won the 1995 Masters

10. Phil Mickelson when he won his first major (2004 Masters)

ANSWERS

1. 21

2. 46

3. 97

4. 2

5. 28

6. 32

7. 28

8. 52

9. 43

10. 33

CHIP SHOT

I played the Tour in 1967 and told jokes and
nobody laughed. Then I won the Open the next year,
told the same jokes, and everybody laughed like hell.

-Lee Trevino

CONTROVERSY!!!

1. In a 2004 book, Ken Venturi stirred up a 46 year old Masters rules controversy involving which golf legend?

2. Who was mildly chastised when jokes attributed to him in a GQ magazine cover story were perceived by some as offensive?

3. Which golfer saw his wife and her parents indicted on federal money laundering charges, though he was not implicated?

4. Who lost a K-Mart endorsement deal after uttering jovial but politically incorrect comments following Tiger Woods' 1997 Masters victory?

5. Why the big fuss over Arnold Palmer's endorsement of the ERC2 driver?

6. Name the CBS golf commentator who was ousted by the network in 1996 for his comment about women's golf—specifically breasts and sexual preference.

7. What was feminist Martha Burk's complaint when she led a fizzled protest at the Masters?

8. What did the federal case *PGA Tour, Inc. vs. Martin* concern?

9. Who missed forcing a playoff at the 1968 Masters due to an incorrect scorecard?

10. Who missed forcing a playoff at the 1957 US Women's Open due to an incorrect scorecard?

ANSWERS

1. Arnold Palmer

2. Tiger Woods

3. John Daly

4. Fuzzy Zoeller

5. It is banned by the USGA.

6. Ben Wright

7. The prohibition of female members at Augusta

8. Whether disabled golfer Casey Martin should be permitted to use a cart during competition in PGA Tour events

9. Roberto Di Vicenzo (Bob Goalby won.)

10. Jackie Pung (Betsy Rawls won.)

CHIP SHOT

Golf is essentially an exercise in masochism conducted out of doors.

-Paul O'Neil

AUGUSTA

1. Which long deceased golf legend still holds the title of Augusta National President in Perpetuity?

2. What major US Army installation is located near Augusta?

3. What building does the solid silver Masters trophy depict?

4. Which of the following was never a member of Augusta National: Warren Buffett, Howard Hughes, E. F. Hutton or Ty Cobb?

5. What was the Masters originally known as?

6. The course was temporarily closed during World War II. How was all that grass put to use?

7. The paying crowd at the Masters is known not as the gallery, but as what?

8. The reigning Masters champ chooses the menu for the Champions Dinner. Who chose cheeseburgers, fries and milkshakes in 1998?

9. Name the legendary detective agency that traditionally handles security for the Masters.

10. What is the name of Augusta's minor league baseball team?

ANSWERS

1. Bobby Jones

2. Fort Gordon

3. The Augusta National Clubhouse

4. Hughes

5. The Augusta National Invitational

6. Cattle grazing

7. Patrons

8. Tiger Woods

9. Pinkerton's

10. The Augusta Green Jackets
    (a Boston Red Sox A affiliate)

CHIP SHOT

Around the clubhouse they'll tell you even God
has to practice his putting. In fact, even Nicklaus does.

-Jim Murray

NUMBERS

The answers are all numbers.

1. Minimum age requirement when the US Senior Open was established in 1980

2. Age it was lowered to the following year

3. Number of double greens at St. Andrews

4. Number of single greens there

5. An eagle on a par five

6. The number of years the British Open was not played due to World War II

7. Number of clubs permitted in a bag in tournament play by the USGA

8. The depth of the hole in inches

9. Par for the course in tournament play at Augusta National

10. Bobby Jones appeared in the Masters 12 times. What was his lowest 18 hole score?

ANSWERS

1. 55

2. 50

3. 7

4. 4

5. 3

6. 6 (1940-45)

7. 14

8. 4

9. 72

10. 72 (He never broke par.)

CHIP SHOT

Some of these Legends of Golf have been around for
a long time. When they talk about having a good grip,
they're talking about dentures.

-Bob Hope, on the Senior Tour

HOLES

Below are descriptions of fairly well known holes
on famous courses. Name them.

1. A large tree near the 17th is known as "The Eisenhower Tree."

2. The 226 yard 4th has been called a "Texas size par 3."

3. A drive on the 7th at this Birmingham, Michigan course is threatened by bunkers on the left and water on the right.

4. The 4th (a par 3) on this Springfield, New Jersey course was famously reworked by Robert Trent Jones in the mid '50s and features a stone walled pond in front of the green and four bunkers behind it.

5. The 18th fairway at this ancient course is reached by crossing a small stone bridge.

6. The intimidating "Church Pews" bunker lies between the 3rd and 4th fairways.

7. The 7th features "Hell's Half Acre," the world's largest sand trap as documented by the *Guinness Book of World Records.*

8. The 625 yard 16th on the South Course at this Akron club, one of the longest par 5s anywhere, doglegs from right to left and has a large lake in front of the green.

9. The tiny 126 yard 8th is known as the "Postage Stamp."

10. The 17th green sits on a clifftop high above the water at this California public course.

ANSWERS

1. Augusta National
2. Colonial
3. Oakland Hills
4. Baltusrol
5. St. Andrews
6. Oakmont
7. Pine Valley
8. Firestone
9. Royal Troon
10. Pebble Beach

CHIP SHOT

Golf fairways should be made more narrow.
Then everyone would have to play from the rough,
not just me.

-Seve Ballesteros

LOOSER LINKS LINGO

More definitions… This time most are a bit more informal.

1. A tournament in which each player in a group hits a tee shot. The group determines which ball is the best of the group and all players hit from that spot. Play continues in this manner until holing out.

2. A tournament similar to that described above except best ball is played only on the second shot.

3. The dead center of the club head and the most desirable point to hit the ball

4. A second "first" shot, often from the first tee

5. A putt so short that it is conceded by an opponent

6. A betting system in which an equal amount is wagered on the front nine, the back nine and the final score

7. To hit the ball with the part of the club between the head and the shaft

8. A tournament in which each group starts off on a different hole and tees off at the same time

9. A scoring system, often modified, in which points are awarded on each hole for bogies, pars, birdies, etc.

10. A swing that misses the ball completely

ANSWERS

1. Scramble
2. Shamble
3. Sweet Spot
4. Mulligan
5. Gimme
6. Nassau
7. Shank
8. Shotgun
9. Stableford
10. Whiff

CHIP SHOT

Golf is like a puzzle without an answer.

-Gary Player

COLLEGE DAYS

Below are ten pros and ten colleges.
Match each golfer with his alma mater.

1. Phil Mickelson	A. UCLA
2. Jack Nicklaus	B. University of North Carolina
3. Arnold Palmer	C. University of Texas
4. John Daly	D. Arizona State
5. Davis Love III	E. Morgan State
6. Justin Leonard	F. Long Beach State
7. Rocco Mediate	G. Wake Forest
8. Mark O'Meara	H. Florida Southern University
9. Corey Pavin	I. University of Arkansas
10. Jim Thorpe	J. Ohio State

ANSWERS

1. D (Mickelson—Arizona State)

2. J (Nicklaus—Ohio State)

3. G (Palmer—Wake Forest)

4. I (Daly—Arkansas)

5. B (Love—UNC)

6. C (Leonard—Texas)

7. H (Mediate—FSU)

8. F (O'Meara—Long Beach State)

9. A (Pavin—UCLA)

10. E (Thorpe—Morgan State)

CHIP SHOT

I can airmail the ball, but sometimes
I don't get the right address on it.

-Jim Dent

SARTORIAL SPLENDOR

1. Name the quirky golfer who is instantly recognizable by the flipped up bill on his cap.

2. We never see male golfers wearing short pants at tournament events, even on the hottest days. Is this a written or an unwritten rule?

3. The Masters green jacket was introduced in 1949. Who was the first winner to wear it?

4. Is a replica of that famous green jacket available for purchase on the official Masters web site?

5. What common article of clothing did Bobby Jones nearly always wear on the course that virtually no golfer would wear there today?

6. Which golf legend nearly always wore a straw hat when playing, especially in his later years?

7. Which golfer was once sponsored by the National Football League and wore the colors and logos of various teams?

8. With which company's logo is Tiger Woods so strongly associated that he was often seen wearing it in ads for other companies?

9. Why was Ken Venturi wearing sweaty rain pants for two holes during the 1968 Masters?

10. Up-and-comer Charles Howell III has a deal with Swedish designer Johan Lindberg. Which other golfer hooked them up?

ANSWERS

1. Jesper Parnevik

2. Written (USGA, PGA and Royal and Ancient)

3. Sam Snead

4. No

5. A necktie

6. Snead

7. Payne Stewart

8. Nike's

9. He split his pants lining up to putt and had to wait until the turn to change.

10. Who else but Jesper Parnevik?

CHIP SHOT

I played nine holes with the new short-distance ball.
Playing a match with it is like two boxers
fighting with pillows.

-Sam Snead

RELATIVELY SPEAKING

1. What sport did the father of 1967 US Women's Open winner Catherine Lacoste play professionally?

2. Name the uncle of pro Jay Haas who won the Masters.

3. In what "sport" was Babe Didrikson Zaharias' husband George a professional?

4. Are Robert Trent Jones and Robert Tyre Jones related?

5. Name the son of a 20th century entertainment legend who won the US Amateur in 1981.

6. What is J.C. Snead's relation to Sam?

7. Name the golfer who married baseball's Ray Knight in 1981.

8. Name the father and son who won tournaments on the same day in 1999 (the former in a senior event).

9. Name the father and son who dominated the British Open in the early years.

10. The Walker Cup is named for onetime USGA head George Herbert Walker. How is he related to the two Presidents Bush?

ANSWERS

1. Her father was tennis pro Rene Lacoste.

2. Bob Goalby (1968)

3. Wrestling

4. They are not related.

5. Nathaniel Crosby, son of Bing

6. Sam is J. C.'s uncle.

7. Nancy Lopez

8. David Duval won the Players Championship and his father Bob won the Emerald Coast Classic on March 28, 1999.

9. Tom Morris, Senior and Junior

10. Maternal grandfather of Bush (41st president) and great-grandfather of Bush (43rd chief executive)

CHIP SHOT

It wasn't dangerous enough.
I'd rather be in the gallery and get hit by a ball.

-Jerry Seinfeld, on the first round of golf he ever played

BOBBY JONES

In a world without him, golf would be a lot different.
Deserving of a page of his own, here's to asking how much
you know about Bobby Jones.

1. In what city was he born?

2. What was his professional occupation?

3. What did he call his favorite putter?

4. He won an earlier version of golf's Grand Slam. What were
those four events?

5. Name the New York banker with whom he founded
Augusta National.

6. How many US Opens did he win?

7. How many British Opens?

8. What was his total dollar amount of career golf winnings
when he retired from competitive play?

9. What disease left him incapacitated in his later years?

10. In what city did he die?

ANSWERS

1. Atlanta, Georgia

2. Lawyer

3. "Calamity Jane"

4. US Open, British Open, US Amateur and British Amateur

5. Clifford Roberts

6. Four

7. Three

8. Zero… He never turned pro.

9. Severe arthritis

10. Atlanta, Georgia

CHIP SHOT

There are no mulligans in that sport.

-Gary Player, about bungee jumping

WHO WAS THAT GUY?

1. Who won the Greater Greensboro Open eight times, a record for winning the same PGA Tour event?

2. Who was the only player to win the PGA twice in the '80s?

3. Who captained the US Ryder Cup Team from 1927-37?

4. Who won the US Open in 1986 on his 23rd try?

5. Who was the golf legend honored by the US Post Office with a stamp in 1981?

6. Who won the US Amateur in 1974 and the US Open two years later?

7. Who held the lead in all four majors in 1986 going into the final round yet won only the British Open?

8. Horace Smith (obviously) and Gene Sarazen won the first two Masters, both as first time participants. Who was the next to win the tournament on his first try?

9. Who won the Northern Telecom Open in 1991 as an amateur and in 1995 as a pro?

10. Who was known for adopting an unorthodox croquet-style putting stance on short putts that was later prohibited?

ANSWERS

1. Sam Snead

2. Larry Nelson

3. Walter Hagen

4. Raymond Floyd

5. Bobby Jones

6. Jerry Pate

7. Greg Norman

8. Fuzzy Zoeller (1979)

9. Phil Mickelson

10. Sam Snead

CHIP SHOT

Learning to play golf is like learning to play the violin.
It's not only difficult to do,
it's very painful to everyone around you.

-Hal Linden

RESPECT YOUR ELDERS

Put the following in the order of the year
born, starting with the oldest.

1. Jack Nicklaus

2. Byron Nelson

3. Arnold Palmer

4. Phil Mickelson

5. Tiger Woods

6. Sergio Garcia

7. John Daly

8. Billy Casper

9. Michelle Wie

10. Nancy Lopez

ANSWERS

1. Nelson (born 1912)

2. Palmer (1929)

3. Casper (1931)

4. Nicklaus (1941)

5. Lopez (1957)

6. Daly (1966)

7. Mickelson (1970)

8. Woods (1975)

9. Garcia (1980)

10. Wie (1989)

CHIP SHOT

Golf and women are a lot alike. You know you are not going to wind up with anything but grief, but you can't resist the impulse.

-Jackie Gleason

CAN I GET A RULING?

Give us the official ruling for each of the following.

1. I make several footprints in a bunker while looking for my ball. Can my caddy rake them out before I take my shot?

2. My ball is a couple of inches from a divot hole. Can I replace the nearby divot before I shoot?

3. My ball is next to a tree. Can I hit it left-handed with a right-handed club?

4. I take the pin out and tap in with one hand while still holding the pin. Is this OK?

5. My ball just rolled out of sight down a drainpipe. What do I do?

6. My ball is about a foot from a gate on a fence bordering other property. Can I open the gate for a little elbow room?

7. The caddy lost my putter. Can I replace it during the round?

8. Can I use a little billiards chalk on my 7-iron?

9. I was trying out a new putter earlier. For convenience I put it in my bag with my other 14 clubs. It's there for the entire round, but I never touch it. Is this OK?

10. Can I remove an anthill from the green?

ANSWERS

1. Yes (as long as it doesn't improve my lie)

2. Yes

3. Yes (as long as the club head strikes the ball)

4. Yes

5. Place a new ball closest to the spot where the original ball entered the drainpipe.

6. No

7. No

8. No

9. No

10. Yes

CHIP SHOT

He has won almost as much money playing golf as I've spent on lessons.

-Bob Hope, on Arnold Palmer

CAN I GET A RULING? II

1. How long can I search for a lost ball until it is declared officially lost?

2. How long can I wait for an overhanging ball to fall into the cup?

3. I can't find my ball after an approach shot to the green so I play another and score a triple bogey. I then discover that my original ball was in the cup all along. Which score counts?

4. Can I spit on the ball a little before teeing off?

5. A pine cone blew across the green and knocked my ball in. Does it count?

6. Can I carry my weight training club in my bag for the round with the rest of my clubs?

7. A hawk swoops down and scoops up a moving ball I just putted and flies off with it. What do I do?

8. It's raining. Can my caddy hold an umbrella over me while I putt?

9. Can I hold my own umbrella and make a one handed short putt?

10. A divot just landed near my ball. Can I remove it?

ANSWERS

1. Five minutes

2. Ten seconds

3. The first. The hole was completed when the first ball went in.

4. No

5. No. The ball is replaced without penalty.

6. Only if the total is 14 or fewer, counting the weight training club

7. Replace it at the original spot and putt again without penalty.

8. No

9. No

10. Yes

CHIP SHOT

Golf practice: something you do to convert a nasty hook into a wicked slice.

-Henry Beard

CAN I GET A RULING? III

One more time. What is the official ruling?

1. As I'm swinging the club, the wind blows the ball off the tee and I miss it. Does the stroke count?

2. I swing and miss an approach shot. Does it count as a stroke?

3. I broke my 7-iron in a hissy fit and finished without one. I learn I'll be in a playoff. Can I get a new one?

4. Before I even tee it up, on the first tee I snap off a tree branch that might have interfered with my swing. Is this OK?

5. Can I hot dog it up a bit and hole a short putt billiard-style with the opposite end of the putter?

6. The caddy trips and accidentally breaks my driver before I tee off. Can I replace it?

7. I haven't teed off yet and I run into a player who has just finished. Can I ask him what club to hit on the third hole?

8. My ball lands next to a dead mouse in a bunker. Can I remove the mouse?

9. I'm disqualified during a playoff. Does this apply to the entire tournament?

10. Can I remove an out-of-bounds stake that interferes with my swing?

ANSWERS

1. Yes
2. Yes
3. Yes
4. No
5. No
6. Yes
7. Yes. The round hasn't started.
8. No
9. No. Only for the playoff
10. No

CHIP SHOT

Mulligan: invented by an Irishman
who wanted to hit one more 20-yard grounder.

-Jim Bishop

PUTTER POTPOURRI

1. Name the golf legend, often credited with ensuring that the sport would be a "gentleman's game," who was once known for his horrible temper.

2. What is the Scottish word for "piece of turf?"

3. Which Pennsylvania course claims to be the oldest continuously operating golf course in the USA?

4. A US Open practice round at Oakmont in 1994 was the first time Jack Nicklaus and Arnold Palmer played in the same group there in 32 years. What were the circumstances of that previous pairing?

5. Name the event, originally played in non-Ryder Cup years, that pits a USA team against an international one.

6. What was the social significance of Pete Brown's victory at the 1964 Waco Turner Open?

7. When was *The Golfer*, the first American periodical devoted to golf first published—1894, 1920, 1929 or 1945?

8. At what Florida facility is the World Golf Hall of Fame located?

9. What is "Give me a Laurel and Hardy" in golfspeak?

10. On which four days of the week is a golf tournament usually played?

ANSWERS

1. Bobby Jones

2. Divot

3. Foxburg Country Club, Foxburg, PA (founded 1887)

4. A playoff round for the 1962 US Open Championship

5. The President's Cup

6. He was the first black player to win a PGA event.

7. 1894

8. World Golf Village

9. "Give me a 10 on that hole."

10. Thursday through Sunday

CHIP SHOT

If you think your hands are more important in your golf
swing than your legs, try walking a hole on your hands.

-Gary Player

PAR THREES

1. At which venue did Jack Nicklaus win the Tournament of Champions in 1971, 1973 and 1977?

2. Name the three "Opens" won by Lee Trevino in 1971.

3. Who was Sporting News Man of the Year, *Sports Illustrated* Sportsman of the Year and AP Male Athlete of the Year for 1971?

4. Who topped the US money list in 1986, 1990 and 1995?

5. Who won British Opens in three decades (1959, 1968 and 1974)?

6. Where are the 11th, 12th and 13th holes known as the "Amen Corner?"

7. From 1960 to 1966 only three men won the Masters. Name the three.

8. Who were the three players tied at the end of regulation at the 1994 US Open at Oakmont?

9. Name the first three golfers to win a million dollars.

10. Name the three players struck by lightning at the 1975 Western Open.

ANSWERS

1. La Costa

2. US, British and Canadian

3. Lee Trevino

4. Greg Norman

5. Gary Player

6. Augusta National

7. Arnold Palmer ('60, '62 and '64), Jack Nicklaus ('63, '65 and '66) and Gary Player ('61)

8. Ernie Els, Loren Roberts and Colin Montgomerie

9. Palmer, Player and Nicklaus

10. Lee Trevino, Jerry Heard and Bobby Nichols

CHIP SHOT

Playing golf is like raising children.
You keep thinking you'll do better next time.

-E.C. Mckenzie

TOURNAMENT TALK

1. Here in the colonies we call it the British Open. What is the official name?

2. Which three tournaments are known as the "Triple Crown of Golf?"

3. Name the PGA event which began with a Jack Nicklaus win in 1974, has been called the "fifth major?"

4. Which of the following once hosted an eponymous Pro-Am: Alan Alda, Mike Farrell, Jamie Farr or McLean Stevenson?

5. The Bob Hope Desert Classic continues today under what name?

6. What show biz legend founded what is now known as the AT&T Pebble Beach National Pro-Am?

7. Which women's major is played at Mission Hills Country Club?

8. Who was the founder of the original version of that tournament?

9. Where was the World Series of Golf played through 1998?

10. What is the permanent home of the World Matchplay Championship?

ANSWERS

1. The Open Championship
2. The US, British and Canadian Opens
3. The Players Championship
4. Farr
5. Bob Hope Chrysler Classic
6. Bing Crosby
7. The Nabisco Championship
8. Dinah Shore
9. Firestone
10. England's Wentworth Golf Club

CHIP SHOT

Having a great golf swing helps under pressure, but golf is a game about scoring. It's like an artist who can get a two-inch brush at Wal-Mart for 20 cents or a fine camel-hair brush from an art store for 20 dollars. The brush doesn't matter - how the finished painting looks is what matters.

-Jerry Pate

THE TROPHY CASE

1. At which tournament does the winner receive the Dinah Shore Trophy?

2. Who won the *Sports Illustrated* 20th Century Sports Award (for individual sports, men) in 1999?

3. For whom is the PGA Player of the Year award named?

4. How does a player win a crystal vase at the Masters?

5. Name the team competition involving women amateurs from the USA and Great Britain that began in 1932.

6. With what award did President Bush present Arnold Palmer in 2004?

7. What is the Vardon Trophy awarded for?

8. What is the Vare Trophy awarded for?

9. How many teams compete for the Ryder Cup?

10. What is the award given to the PGA Tour's leading money winner called?

ANSWERS

1. The Dinah Shore Trophy

2. Jack Nicklaus

3. It is called the Jack Nicklaus Trophy.

4. By posting the day's lowest score

5. Curtis Cup

6. Presidential Medal of Freedom

7. PGA lowest scoring average

8. LPGA lowest scoring average

9. Two (American and European)

10. Arnold Palmer Award

CHIP SHOT

A golfer is someone with hoof and mouth disease.
He hoofs it all day and mouths it all night.

-Will Rogers

DEUCES

1. Who both went 17 straight years with at least one PGA Tour victory?

2. Which two legends each won five PGA events in 1971?

3. Which two guys won 11 and 12 PGA titles, respectively, the last three years of the '90s?

4. When did Nick Faldo win back-to-back Masters, both in playoffs?

5. Name the only two players in PGA history with wins that straddle four decades.

6. What USC golfer was NCAA champ in 1976 and 1977?

7. Name the duo who took home the EMC World Cup for the USA four years running (1992-95)?

8. Which two legends previously teamed to win that event for the USA in 1963, 1964, 1966 and 1967?

9. The two lowest 18 hole rounds at Pebble Beach, both 10-under 62s, were shot in 1983 and 1997. Name the two record holders.

10. Name the two brothers who each won his first PGA Senior event (2000 and 2001).

ANSWERS

1. Jack Nicklaus (1962-78) and Arnold Palmer (1955-71)

2. Nicklaus and Lee Trevino

3. David Duval and Tiger Woods

4. 1989 and 1990

5. Sam Snead ('30s-'60s) and Raymond Floyd ('60s-'90s)

6. Scott Simpson

7. Fred Couples and Davis Love III

8. Who else but Jack and Arnie

9. Tom Kite (1983) and David Duval (1997)

10. Lanny (Ace Group Classic) and Bobby (Lightpath Long Island Classic) Wadkins

CHIP SHOT

You have to put your putter out to pasture every so often, let it eat and get fat so it can get more birdies.

-Greg Norman

FOR SENIORS ONLY

1. Where was the first Senior Open held?

2. Name the 60 year old who won the 2000 Cadillac/NFL Golf Classic.

3. How about the 62 year old who won the 1998 Northville Long Island Classic?

4. Who was the first winner of a PGA Senior Tour Event (1980 Atlantic City International)?

5. What is the award for the lowest scoring average on the Senior Tour called?

6. What is the award for the Senior Tour's leading money winner called?

7. Who was the Senior Tour Player of the Year for 1995 and 1996?

8. How about for 1997 and 1998?

9. Who was the first to win his first two Senior Tour events?

10. Who was the first to reach 30 Senior Tour wins?

ANSWERS

1. Winged Foot

2. Lee Trevino

3. Gary Player

4. Don January

5. The Byron Nelson Award

6. The Arnold Palmer Award (same as the PGA)

7. Jim Colbert

8. Hale Irwin

9. Bruce Fleisher (Royal Carribean Classic and American Express Classic in 1999)

10. Hale Irwin

CHIP SHOT

How long does John Daly drive a golf ball?
When I was a kid, I didn't go that far on vacation.

-Chi Chi Rodriguez

WHO WAS THAT GUY—OR GAL?

1. Who won every "skin" for an even million bucks at the 2001 Skins Game?

2. Who was the first to break 60 at a sanctioned PGA Tour Event (1977)?

3. Who became the first to successfully defend a US Open title since Ben Hogan did in 1950-51?

4. Who became the oldest rookie ever on the PGA Tour at age 47 in 1996?

5. Tiger Woods was the PGA's leading money winner in 1997, 1999, 2000 and 2001. Who was Mr. Moneybags in 1998?

6. Who was the first Augusta, Georgia, native to win the Masters?

7. Who won the British Open three times in the '50s (as well as once in the '40s)?

8. Who won the PGA in 1968 to become the oldest winner of a major at age 48?

9. Who was the Australian who finished first or second in seven straight British Opens?

10. Who had a hole-in-one at the 1959 US Women's Open?

ANSWERS

1. Greg Norman

2. Al Geiberger with a 59 at the Danny Thomas Memphis Classic

3. Curtis Strange (1988-89)

4. Allen Doyle

5. David Duval

6. Larry Mize (1987)

7. Bobby Locke (1949, 1950, 1952 and 1957)

8. Julius Boros

9. Peter Thomson (1952-58)

10. Patty Berg

CHIP SHOT

On the golf course, a man may be the dogged victim of inexorable fate, be struck down by an appalling stroke of tragedy, become the hero of unbelievable melodrama, or the clown in a side-splitting comedy.

-Bobby Jones

IT'S IN THE BAG

1. Which well known sporting goods company was the first in the US to manufacture golf clubs?

2. Who was the first pro to found a company selling clubs under his name?

3. During which decade did metal shafts almost completely replace wooden ones—'20s, '30s, '40s or '50s?

4. What was patented in 1899 by George Grant, a Boston dentist?

5. What now standard feature on the surface of golf balls was first introduced in 1880?

6. Who is credited with inventing the sand wedge?

7. What's the diameter of a golf ball: 1.68", 1.48", 1.28" or 1.08"?

8. King James IV of Scotland commissioned a Perth bowmaker to fashion a set of clubs. This is the first historical reference to custom clubs. Was it 1502, 1602, 1702 or 1802?

9. When was the "Big Bertha" club introduced—1985, 1987, 1989 or 1981?

10. What is a *featherie*?

ANSWERS

1. A. G. Spaulding and Brothers (1894)

2. Walter Hagen (1922)

3. '30s

4. The golf tee

5. "Dimples"

6. Gene Sarazen

7. 1.68"

8. 1502

9. 1991

10. A golf ball used until about 1850, the featherie was a leather sack filled with wet goose feathers. As the feathers dried, they expanded and made the ball hard.

CHIP SHOT

The game was easy for me as a kid.
I had to play a while to find out how hard it is.

-Raymond Floyd

MONIKERS

Can you identify the following from their nicknames?

1. Big Momma

2. Boom Boom

3. Lord Byron

4. Slammin' Sammy

5. Champagne Tony

6. Mr. X

7. Super Mex

8. El Nino

9. Radar

10. Wild Thing

ANSWERS

1. Joanne Carner

2. Fred Couples

3. Byron Nelson

4. Sam Snead

5. Tony Lema

6. Miller Barber

7. Lee Trevino

8. Sergio Garcia

9. Mike Reid

10. John Daly

CHIP SHOT

Golf is a game where the ball always lies poorly
and the player well.

-Ben Polish

FIRST OF ALL—
SECOND TIME AROUND

1. Who won the first (and second) World Series of Golf?

2. Where did the first miniature golf course open in 1916?

3. It's better known for tennis, but how was amateur golf history made at Wimbledon, England in 1878?

4. Who was the first to win over two million dollars in official prize money in a single season?

5. Which golf legend helped design a golf course in China?

6. Who was the first to score 20-under in 72 holes at an LPGA event?

7. What significant (now common) "first" was established at the 1933 Hershey Open?

8. Who was the first black golfer to play on a US Ryder Cup Team?

9. When did the Ryder Cup first include players from the European mainland?

10. When was the first sudden death playoff in a major?

ANSWERS

1. Jack Nicklaus

2. Pinehurst, North Carolina

3. It was the site of the first university golf competition (won by Oxford).

4. Tiger Woods, in 1997

5. Arnold Palmer (Zhangshan Hot Springs Resort)

6. Nancy Lopez (a 268 at the 1986 Henredon Classic)

7. It was the first corporate sponsored and titled pro tournament (Hershey Chocolate Company).

8. Lee Elder in 1979

9. 1979

10. The 1977 PGA at Pebble Beach when Lanny Wadkins beat Gene Littler on the third playoff hole

CHIP SHOT

In case you don't know very much about the game of golf, a good one-iron shot is about as easy to come by as an understanding wife.

-Dan Jenkins

A SIMPLE YES OR NO WILL DO

1. Didn't Augusta National once host the US Open?

2. Did Chi Chi Rodriguez ever win a major?

3. Did Ben Hogan ever compete at St. Andrews?

4. Did anyone win the Masters both before and after the years it was not played during World War II (1943-45)?

5. How about the US Open (1942-45)?

6. Was the PGA ever canceled during World War II?

7. Was golf ever an Olympic sport?

8. Is it true that there have been less than a dozen holes-in-one made yearly on the PGA tour over the last 25 years?

9. Did Arnold Palmer win the most majors in the '60s?

10. Did tennis great Althea Gibson ever play on the LPGA Tour?

ANSWERS

1. No

2. No

3. No

4. Yes (Jimmy Demaret in 1940 and 1947)

5. No

6. Yes (in 1943 only)

7. Yes (in 1900 and 1904)

8. No (not since there were only ten in 1971)

9. No—He won six to Jack Nicklaus's seven.

10. Yes, from 1963-77 (Her best year was 1967, 23rd on the money list.)

CHIP SHOT

I've lost 2,000 pounds, but I've gained 2,200.

-Billy Casper, on his personal "Battle of the Bulge"

THEY DON'T (NECESSARILY) PLAY THE GAME

They are well known in the world of golf,
but not as players (though they may hit a few now and then).
Can you identify the following?

1. Karsten Solheim

2. Nathaniel "Iron Man" Avery

3. Ivor Robson

4. Butch Harmon

5. Harvey Penick

6. Pete Dye

7. Michael "Fluff" Cowan

8. William "Hootie" Johnson

9. Alister MacKenzie

10. Dr. Bob Rotella

ANSWERS

1. Creator of Ping golf clubs

2. Arnold Palmer's caddy during his glory years

3. The announcer who calls each player's name from the first tee at the British Open (since 1974)

4. Golf coach who has worked with Tiger Woods, Greg Norman and Davis Love III, among others

5. Noted golf writer and coach

6. Course architect who has designed over 70 challenging courses

7. Tiger Woods' caddy when he first turned pro; also caddied for Peter Jacobson and Michelle Wie

8. Chairman of Augusta National

9. Course architect best known for designing Augusta National with Bobby Jones

10. University of Virginia sports psychologist who has worked with Pat Bradley, Brad Faxon and Nick Price

CHIP SHOT

If it weren't for golf, I'd probably be a caddie today.

-George Archer

GOLF GROANERS

As we're nearing the nineteenth ho-ho-hole,
test your knowledge of these Q & A's.

1. Why is golf a lot like taxes?

2. Why do most golfers use carts instead of caddies?

3. What did the ancient Romans yell on the golf course?

4. How is a wedding ring like a bag of golf clubs?

5. How many golfers does it take to screw in a light bulb?

6. What was the title of the book about the Siamese twins'
   golfing experiences?

7. Why can't we tell you the one about the golfer who
   lost 288 balls?

8. What goes putt, putt, putt?

9. What's it called when you purchase a set of clubs at
   list price?

10. What's a golfer's favorite soft drink?

ANSWERS

1. You drive very hard to get to the green only to wind up in a hole.

2. Because you can count on your cart but it can't count on you.

3. "IV!"

4. Both are instruments of eternal servitude.

5. Two. One to do it and another to tell him he looked up.

6. *Tee for Two*

7. It's too gross.

8. A lousy golfer

9. Getting shafted

10. Slice

LAST OF ALL

What was the last major won by each of the following?
The year is provided.

1. Lee Trevino (1984)

2. Sam Snead (1954)

3. Gene Sarazen (1935)

4. Gary Player (1978)

5. Arnold Palmer (1964)

6. Jack Nicklaus (1986)

7. Byron Nelson (1945)

8. Johnny Miller (1976)

9. Walter Hagen (1929)

10. Billy Casper (1970)

ANSWERS

1. Trevino—PGA

2. Snead—Masters

3. Sarazen—Masters

4. Player—Masters

5. Palmer—Masters

6. Nicklaus—Masters

7. Nelson—PGA

8. Miller—British Open

9. Hagen—British Open

10. Casper—Masters

CHIP SHOT

After an abominable round of golf, a man is known
to have slit his wrists with a razor blade and, having
bandaged them, to have stumbled into the locker room
and inquired of his partner, "What time tomorrow?"

-Alistair Cooke

TICKLES AT THE TURN

Enjoy a few one-liners from
the late great Bob Hope about his favorite sport.

"I was Spiro Agnew's partner one day at Palm Springs, although I didn't realize it until my caddie handed me a blindfold and a cigarette."

"Whenever I play with Jerry Ford, I usually try to make it a foursome — the President, myself, a paramedic and a faith healer."

"Gerald Ford—the man who made golf a contact sport."

"Jimmy Stewart could have been a good golfer, but he speaks so slowly that by the time he yells 'Fore!' the guy he's hit is already in an ambulance on the way to the hospital."

"I set out to play golf with the intention of shooting my age, but I shot my weight instead."

"Golf is my profession. Show business is just to pay the green fees."

"Incidentally, the toughest part of the course for me nowadays are the sand traps. It's not hard to get the ball out....the problem, at my age, is to get me out."

"I asked my good friend, Arnold Palmer how I could improve my game. He advised me to cheat."

"The Scottish caddies are great. One old fellow at St. Andrews told me, 'I had a golfer who was so lousy he threw his clubs into the water. Then he dove in himself. I thought he was going to drown, but I remembered he couldn't keep his head down long enough.'"

"I've played some strange rounds of golf in my travels. One course in Alaska was hacked out of the wilderness. My caddy was a moose. Every time I reached for a club he thought I was trying to steal his antlers."

And now this book concludes
with some appropriate inspiration...

The Golfer's Prayer

Now I Lay Me Down To Sleep

I Pray The Lord My Life To Keep

Though I Know You'll Eventually Take My Soul

Please Let Me Prepare At The 19th Hole!

THE BATHROOM LIBRARY

The Bathroom Trivia Book

The Bathroom Joke Book

The Bathroom Game Book

The Bathroom Sports Quiz Book

The Bathroom Super Bowl Quiz Book

The Bathroom Baseball Book

The Bathroom Golf Book

The Bathroom Gambling Book